Powerful Prophetic Proclamations

*Taking possession
through writing and speaking out
positive declarations*

Declarations are written by Kathy DeGraw
Copyright © 2017 Kathy DeGraw

Published by K Publishing

Unless otherwise indicated, all Scriptures are taken from the Holy Bible, New King James Version (NKJV) ®. Copyright © 1982 by Thomas Nelson. Used by permission. All rights reserved.

Scriptures noted (MEV) are taken from the Holy Bible, the Modern English Version. Copyright © 2014 by Military Bible Association. Published and distributed by Charisma House.

Cover design by Emcat Designs
Facebook: Emcat Designs
Email: Megparker1990@gmail.com

Dedication

I DEDICATE THIS BOOK to my Father in heaven who has given me all wisdom to prophetically write what the Spirit of the Lord is saying, and, to you, the reader, that it may empower you to speak out simple statements and prophetic proclamations to release your destiny.

Table of Contents

Introduction 7
How to Make Your Prayers More Powerful 9
Abundance of Heaven 11
Abundance 12
Acceptance—I Am Accepted!. 13
Flesh Submission 21
Faith—I Am in Faith!. 22
Blessings. 29
Call Forth Good Things! 30
Calling Forth New 31
Change 32
Renewal and Change in a Person 33
New Year ~ New Season 34
Command Your Day! 45
Crying Out for More 46
Morning Declaration 47
Daily Release 48
Family and Home Blessings 56
Family Unity 58
College Student 59
I Am Blessed! 69

I Am Not Defeated! 70
I Have a Sound Mind 71
I Have the Power 72
I Speak Life 73
I Trust 74
Peace 75
Anointing Wisdom I Claim, Call Forth and Release 82
I Am Will Accept My Assignment! 83
Kingdom Destiny 84
Spouse's Ministry Assignment 86
Meetings 87
Kingdom Faith 88
Health ~ Healing 94
Physical Healing 95
Infertility 97
Finances 104
Tithe/Offering by Pastor Ron DeGraw 105
Sale of a Home 106
Powerful Prophetic Saturation 119
Releasing the Past 120
Prophetic Fulfillment Come Forth! 121
Victorious! 122
Worship 128
Widespread Declaration 129
About the Author 137

Introduction

WE'VE ALL HEARD about the power of positive thinking, but what about *positive speaking*? The Bible instructs us in many different passages about our words. Prayer, when spoken out loud into the atmosphere, has powerful results. Jesus spoke out many things, and He experienced nature, people, sickness and demons responding to what He spoke out.

Now is the time for us to speak out and have things in the natural react to what we have spoken out in the spiritual. The idea of this book is to get you to prophetically declare positive things over your life and to have you writing your own prophetic proclamations.

In this book, I have provided prophetic proclamations which you can declare out loud and call forth those things that do not exist in the natural. By speaking them out into the atmosphere, you will discover your faith will increase and your circumstances will change.

I also want to empower you to write your own proclamations for situations that need attention in your life. I have included a set of blank pages behind the sections of declarations. These blank pages start with thought-provoking questions in order to assist you in writing your own declaration. I have also included blank pages in order for you to use your discernment or to allow the Holy Spirit to speak to you.

I have already written two books on declaring which may be helpful to you if you don't already have them. My book *SPEAK OUT* teaches you the power of declaring through prayer. It will teach you scripturally how Jesus and the Father declared, break down legalistic thoughts and increase your faith for declaring. In this book, I have outlined the proper order of declaring and different ways to write a declaration. I also have a book titled *Warfare Declarations* in which I have written several spiritual warfare declarations for you to use in your prayer time. I invite you to check out those resources on my website at www.degrawministries.org or Amazon.com.

I hope you will enjoy this book and journal. My intention when writing it was to provide enough space for you to write your own declarations. You can then declare what the Holy Spirit has given you through my writings and add your own for your convenience of taking it with you as your travel, going to a worship event or walking around your home declaring and proclaiming into the spiritual atmosphere.

May you be abundantly blessed with all knowledge through our Lord and may the Holy Spirit co-labor with you as you write your own proclamations!

– Kathy

How to Make Your Prayers More Powerful!

JESUS MADE PRAYER a priority for His life. We read that Jesus spoke to things such as a fig tree (Matthew 21:19), a little girl, saying, *"Arise"* (Mark 5:41), and to a storm, *"...Peace be still"* (Mark 4:39, MEV).

In other words, when Jesus spoke, people, sickness and disease, nature, and the demonic forces responded in obedience. Storms ceased; trees withered; and sickness, disease and the demons left.

Are we praying as Jesus did? Why are we, as Christians, not seeing our prayers answered?

Jesus has given us that same authority (Luke 10:19). Power went forth as Jesus spoke. When He died and was resurrected, He transferred that power and authority to man. That transfer of power is similar to having power of attorney over someone. You have authority over the person's life and situations. Jesus died and gave us His power of authority. As believers, we need to know that we have the authority to speak to our situations.

Proverbs 18:21 (MEV) reads, *"Death and life are in the power of the tongue...."* And in Matthew, Jesus further talks about faith and speaking out: *"So Jesus said to them, 'Because of your unbelief; for assuredly, I say to you, if you have faith as a mustard seed, you will say to this mountain, "Move from here to there," and it will move, and nothing will be impossible for you' "*(Matthew 17:20, MEV). Jesus continually modeled the example of the power of our belief, authority and the words spoken out of our mouth.

Why are most of our prayers in our minds and not speaking out loud as Jesus did? There is a time to pray in our mind and connect spirit to Spirit with the Father. However, there are times when we need to speak out loud and command the spiritual atmosphere to activate on our words. We need to take authority over the spiritual realm, and that is done by speaking out loud so that the spirit realm can hear what we are commanding it to do—just like Jesus did.

If the answers to some of our prayers are not manifesting, what will it hurt to try and pray differently and speak out loud to things as Jesus did?

Abundance of Heaven

I command clarity of mind, vision, and revelation to come and activate!

    I call forth new hope and joy abundantly!

I implore heaven to activate and dispatch angels to my assistance.

    I decree this season will be one of change!

I declare my mind will be renewed to believe and receive.

    I call forth every good and abundant gift from the Father.

I am blessed with every spiritual blessing!

    I am blessed, favored, loved and wanted!

I have an eternal inheritance!

    I claim, call forth and expect these things to manifest in Jesus' name!

Abundance

I call forth the abundant flow of heaven to open!

I say my year, my season will change to benefit the Kingdom!

I proclaim this will be a year of the manifestation of my promises.

I release angels on assignment to carry out their orders for my family and ministry.

I say I will arise and take my rightful place and position in the Kingdom!

I command no more lack and victim mentality!

I call forth my release from familiar spirits and seasons and cycles of depression, in Jesus' name!

I say blessings and favor are my portion!

The King (King Jesus) is exalted through me!

I say my lips and my mouth will glorify the name of the Lord and speak edification!

My promises and my destiny are coming to pass!

Things in my life aren't going to be the same because the word of God is releasing over my life!

I call these things forth to activation in Jesus' name!

Acceptance—I Am Accepted!

God accepts me; therefore, I have no need to be accepted by the world's system and by people's way of thinking.

God is love; therefore, He accepts me, and that is all that matters.

I am chosen and accepted by God.

I will not allow a person's perception of me or rejection displayed towards me to define me.

I carry identification and authority to do spiritual business in the realm of the Spirit.

The devil knows I have been bought with the blood and the anointing I carry, and so do I.

My identity is not what I do. It's not who people say I am. It's who God says I am.

I believe I am accepted in Jesus' name!

Abundance is something we all need to call forth. Where are you lacking? Where do you need to see the abundance of heaven come forth on your behalf? Write your own declaration calling forth what you specifically need in your life.

_____

_____

_____

_____

_____

_____

_____

_____

_____

_____

_____

_____

_____

_____

_____

_____

_____

_____

Powerful Prophetic Declarations

Meditate and seek the Holy Spirit for prophetic direction. What is the Holy Spirit speaking to you in this moment to write out for the abundance He wants to see manifest in your situation?

Powerful Prophetic Declarations

Powerful Prophetic Declarations

Powerful Prophetic Declarations

Powerful Prophetic Declarations

Flesh Submission

Give me a receiving spirit.

Open me up to be honest with myself and others.

I call forth teachable and correctable spirits and souls.

I call forth my will to align with God's will.

I command my flesh to submit to my soul, my soul to submit to my spirit, and my spirit to align with the Holy Spirit.

I call forth oneness; alignment body, mind, soul and spirit.

I call forth the spiritual realm and atmosphere to come into alignment with the Word of God and the will of God.

Open my spirit man to receive from You.

Help me to seek You.

Unify my heart with Yours, Father God.

Help me want what You want, Lord Jesus.

Truly break my heart for what breaks Yours, Holy Spirit.

Give me Your desires, Heavenly Father.

Faith—I Am in Faith!

I will be in faith and not worry.

    I will be in faith and not doubt.

I will be in faith and not fear.

    I will be in faith and not concern.

I will be in faith and not tiredness.

    I will renew my focus and be in faith.

I will concentrate on God and be in faith.

    Freedom is mine. I will be in faith.

I claim and declare out, I will be in faith.

    I am going to live in faith.

I am going to manifest faith.

    I will trust God.

WHEN DECLARING, WE need to bind our flesh and discover what God's will is for our lives. Take a few moments to journal God's will for your life and then turn it into a proclamation.

_____

_____

_____

_____

_____

_____

_____

_____

_____

_____

_____

_____

_____

_____

_____

_____

_____

_____

Powerful Prophetic Declarations

FAITH TO MANIFEST your prayers is a necessity if you are going to be calling forth something that you don't see in the natural. In my book *SPEAK OUT*, I discuss how to overcome doubt, unbelief, legalism and the mindsets you may experience by not being taught about declaring.

Write a declaration based on Scripture and prophetic insights to overcome any faith obstacles and speak it out.

_____

_____

_____

_____

_____

_____

_____

_____

_____

_____

_____

_____

_____

_____

_____

_____

_____

Powerful Prophetic Declarations

Powerful Prophetic Declarations

Powerful Prophetic Declarations

Blessings

May the blessings of the Lord come upon me!

    God bless me in my coming in and going out!

I call forth the blessings and favor of God and man.

    I decree this is my year of Jubilee!

I declare that good things are coming my way!

    I establish every good and perfect gift in my life to manifest.

I proclaim this is the year for my prophetic words to come to pass.

    I command blessings in my workplace, ministry and family.

I say every good thing is coming my way, in Jesus' name!

Call Forth Good Things!

I claim command and decree that I will walk in the authority Jesus has given me.

I proclaim I have been redeemed by the blood of the Lamb, and I receive the liberty He gave me.

I accept the atoning work of the cross and speak that it manifests in my life.

In my life, Lord, may Your name be glorified.

In my words, thoughts and actions may Your name, Lord, be lifted high.

My hope is in the Lord, not in man; the Lord has a strategic plan for me.

Fear and every fiery dart of the enemy will bow at the feet of Jesus, and since Jesus lives in me, I command fear and every demonic spirit to bow and get out of me, in Jesus' name.

No weapon formed against my mind will prosper, in Jesus' name.

I have the mind of Christ. My mind is bound to Christ's way of thinking.

My love, oh, Lord, is for You and Your people.

My old ways are not God's new ways for me, and my old ways are buried and gone.

My mind is steadfast and fixed on You, God, Your ways and Your Word.

I seal myself and my family into the sonship of the kingdom of God.

I say new revelation is coming my way every day to stay.

I seal it all in by the blood of Jesus, in the name of Jesus.

Calling Forth New

I decree and declare new things are coming to pass.

    Old things have passed away.

Old habits, patterns and cycles be gone, in Jesus' name.

    I am moving forward, not going back.

I have a new life, a fresh anointing in the river of God.

    I am going to shine like the Son!

Miracles are coming my way.

    Huge things are manifesting on my behalf.

I love the Lord.

    God works on my behalf.

I have trust—great trust and faith!

    I have the faith of a giant!

I am huge in the spirit realm!

    I accomplish much for the Kingdom.

I have a mighty King.

    King Jesus is working on my behalf.

I am love.

    I am in the Father, and the Father is in me.

It's breakthrough season, and I'm receiving mine, in the name of Jesus.

Change

I declare and decree a new season of refreshing and holy rain to flood into my life.

I expect and prophesy change in my life and for miracles to flood in with an overwhelming abundance.

I speak, call forth and demand change into my life, ministry and family.

I order angels to go forth and activate on my behalf.

I claim that I will seek the Lord at all times and His direction and leading.

I call forth that I will not run ahead of God or walk out of alignment with the will of God.

I say I will quickly obey the instructions of God.

I call forth this declaration to manifest and for me to be obedient to what the Holy Spirit desires, in Jesus' name.

Renewal and Change in a Person

I ask You, Holy Spirit, to come in and convict (person's name) in the way You know he needs conviction.

Help me, Heavenly Father, to take my hands off his inadequacies.

Convict my family member, friend or loved one, Holy Spirit, to seek You.

Father, create in (person's name) a clean heart.

Cleanse him and reveal his secret faults.

Take the blinders off his eyes so he may see the truth.

Open his ears to hear the truth.

I bind a spirit of pride, control, and offense from activating within him while he is in my presence.

Father, break his heart for what breaks Yours.

Have him love like You love.

I decree a change in the person I am declaring for and call forth Holy Spirit conviction and obedience, in Jesus' name.

New Year ~ New Season

I proclaim this is a year of Jubilee for my family.

I declare my assignment will not be interrupted.

The blessing that is established for me will come forth!

I put a demand on my prophecies to come forth!

I call forth a new level of faith activation and impartation.

Finances, come forth!

Divine strategies, manifest!

I will have abundant favor and blessing this year.

I decree a year of open doors, expansion in territory, divine contracts and connections.

Abundant hope and faith, come forth!

Healing, manifest now!

Body, come into alignment now!

Miracles, manifest!

Abundant peace and joy, manifest in Jesus' name.

POSITIVE PROCLAMATIONS ARE powerful! The Bible says, *"Death and life are in the power of the tongue"* (Proverbs 18:21). There is power in positive thoughts and words. Write a proclamation establishing over yourself the power of positivity.

Powerful Prophetic Declarations

THE BIBLE SPEAKS about how we are blessed and how God desires good things for us. Write a proclamation based on Scripture of the blessings the Bible says we can have. If you need help writing a scriptural declaration, refer to my book *SPEAK OUT* where I teach three different ways to write a declaration. One of those ways is based on scripture.

Powerful Prophetic Declarations

Powerful Prophetic Declarations

People often speak negativity out of their mouths, but as we speak life and positive things we will feel uplifted and believe what we speak.

Write a positive proclamation that brings out the life in you.

_____
_____
_____
_____
_____
_____
_____
_____
_____
_____
_____
_____
_____
_____
_____
_____
_____
_____
_____
_____

Powerful Prophetic Declarations

Powerful Prophetic Declarations

Powerful Prophetic Declarations

Powerful Prophetic Declarations

Powerful Prophetic Declarations

Command Your Day!

I will be in health.

    Healing and wholeness will be mine today.

I will have favor in all I do.

    The Kingdom of God will manifest from me.

I will get much accomplished today.

    I proclaim my spiritual walk will ignite to a new level today.

I command no distractions, delays or detours.

    I call forth productivity for my day and agenda.

I invite the Holy Spirit to invade my day.

    I say the promises of heaven are mine today, in Jesus' name.

Crying Out for More

I claim, command and decree that people would be hungry for You, God.

I say Your people would awaken to desperation for more of You.

I call forth that people would desire to know the depths of Your love and greatness.

I speak that people would want to know the truths of Your beloved Son Jesus and how He intercedes for them.

I pray, Heavenly Father, for the victim mentality, inadequacies and lack of self-worth to fall off people and dissipate, in Jesus' name.

I call forth a remnant of people who will rise and seek Your face, who are so desperate for You that they can't get enough.

I call forth a remnant of people who desire to experience a change in their life and the life of others and will do anything necessary to obtain it.

Morning Declaration

No weapon formed against me will prosper.

I will have favor in the sight of God and man.

I abolish any assignments set against me this day, in Jesus' name.

I call forth an abundance of heavenly rain and divine appointments in my life today.

I say the fruit of the Spirit and the gifts of the Spirit will manifest out of me today.

I will prosper in all I set my hands to and God's word will prosper out of me.

Fear will not come from me, but great faith.

God's plan for my life will prosper, and my prophetic destiny will be set forth into action!

I seal this declaration in by the precious blood of the Lamb in the name of Yeshua Messiah, the Jehovah-Nissi, who is the Lord my banner.

Daily Release

I declare a prophetic release over my day.

I release the joy of the Lord into my life today.

I release the prosperity, increase, abundance of heaven over my life, family, job and ministry.

I render and call forth the heavens to open on my behalf.

I proclaim favor will be my portion today.

I command clarity, focus and clear vision for the plans and purposes of God in my life.

I say health and healing, the blood of Jesus flow through my veins bringing purity, health and abundant life.

I proclaim only Godly, edifying words will be released from my mouth.

There will be no contaminates in my soul because I release angels on assignment to reverse and destroy assignments of the enemy.

I call forth my dreams and desires to manifest.

This will be a day of focus, accomplishments and tasks completed.

I abolish all distractions on my day and cover my day in the blood of Christ and dispatch angels to war and activate on my behalf.

In the mighty name of Jesus, I seal this declaration prayer in and call it forth in the precious name of Yeshua Messiah!

Powerful Prophetic Declarations

Taking authority over the beginning of your day can and will eliminate distractions. When you are focused, you don't need unexpected interruptions. Write a declaration using the facts of the distractions you receive typically and turn the situation around by declaring against them.

_____
_____
_____
_____
_____
_____
_____
_____
_____
_____
_____
_____
_____
_____
_____
_____
_____

Powerful Prophetic Declarations

The Bible contains many references to rising early and spending time with the Lord the first thing in the morning. Write out how you will spend your mornings and then do it!

Powerful Prophetic Declarations

Powerful Prophetic Declarations

Powerful Prophetic Declarations

Powerful Prophetic Declarations

Family and Home Blessings

I declare the holiness of the Lord will reside in my home.

I say there are open heavens over my household.

In Jesus' name, my home will reside in the peace of Jehovah-shalom, the God of peace.

Yahweh is the Master of my home.

The Messiah, the Anointed One, establishes my home.

I proclaim that all of the members of my household serve Yeshua.

The glory of the Lord resides within my home.

My home and family is a place where all are welcome to reside and find solace, refuge and sanctuary.

I speak life to all members of my household and everyone who enters my home; I prophesy to their dry bones, and I say, "Arise and live!"

My family stands on the Word of God, and the Word of God goes out of our mouths and lives in all we do.

My family and my home is a temple of the Lord; we are willing vessels ready and able to be used by Him.

The Lord is my instructor.

My home does not fear man, but the Lord.

As for me and my house, we shall serve the Lord.

My family shall live in unity, love, cooperation, grace and mercy.

Angels are dispatched to my home and family to guard and protect; they are activated on their assignment!

The blood of Jesus is on my doorposts, windows, entryways and exits and is applied to my household and family, vehicles, appliances, yard and property.

I belong to the Lord, and therefore, my family belongs to the Kingdom. I call them in and seal them into a right relationship with Jesus.

I call forth the glory of the Lord to saturate my house, so people are changed as they enter into His presence in my home.

I restrict the enemy from wreaking havoc in my home.

Fire of God, permeate my home and family and burn up anything unclean and negative.

I say the presence of the Lord resides here because it resides within us since the kingdom is within us.

Every good thing according to God's will shall manifest in my home.

Prophetic words come forth for those in my family!

I say we shall prosper (succeed) in all we do!

My family shall bear much great fruit!

The gifts are activated in my family.

My family worships the great I AM, the great Lord Jesus Christ!

I call forth this declaration, in Jesus' name!

Family Unity

Holy Spirit, open the eyes of my spouse to see and know the truth of who I am.

Holy Spirit, convict my spouse, reveal his sin and inadequacies to him to bring forth change through Your correction and direction.

I call forth unity in my home! I proclaim the love of God to saturate us and fill us to overflowing. I declare we will fulfill our calling jointly and individually.

Holy Spirit, convict me to war for my spouse.

I thank You, Lord, that a three-fold cord is not quickly broken and that You are the center of us.

I call forth and proclaim change in my spouse!

I say my family will serve and love the Lord!

I proclaim that my family will be filled with the knowledge of His will in all wisdom and spiritual understanding.

I call forth that my family will walk worthy of the Lord, fully pleasing to Him, being fruitful and faithful in every good work.

I say my family will increase in the knowledge of God and be in obedience and discipline to His Word and His will for their lives.

I speak that my family will be strengthened with all might according to His glorious power!

College Student

I declare and decree for college debt to be supernaturally paid in full.

I proclaim my students will learn with ease, and it will ignite them to study and retain information.

I call forth angels to protect and guard them in all that they do and everywhere they go.

I ask you, God, to send forth the perfect spouse that You have chosen for them.

Align their will with Your will.

I proclaim they will earn the grades needed to keep scholarships active and make learning easy.

I command that You give them favor with professors, students, friends, jobs and everything they need.

I call forth unity in relationships and roommates.

I say they will prosper and receive solid, high-paying jobs directly out of college in the region they are seeking.

Bless them, Father God; let Your hand of protection be upon them.

Keep them on the path You have destined, in Jesus' name.

Reflect on the past dissension that has been in your home. Where do you need to be on the offense instead of the defense? Write an offensive declaration to combat the past warfare you have experienced and to call your family, children or spouse into unity with the word of God.

My thoughts on what I should declare against:

POWERFUL PROPHETIC DECLARATIONS

Declaration for My Family

Powerful Prophetic Declarations

Declaration for My Spouse

Declaration for My Children

Declaration for My Son

Powerful Prophetic Declarations

Declaration for My Daughter

Powerful Prophetic Declarations

POWERFUL PROPHETIC DECLARATIONS

Declaration for Myself
What I need to call forth and change

I Am Blessed!

I will walk in my God-given destiny.

My prophecies are coming forth, speedily and according to God's will.

I walk in my God-given authority!

No weapon formed against me will prosper!

I will have life and live it abundantly!

My life will produce great fruit for the Kingdom!

God blesses me and shows me great favor.

I am blessed in my coming and going.

All things are under my feet.

I walk in prosperity and am rich in the Word!

I have blessings in abundance flowing through me.

I am a blessing to all I come in contact.

I share the love of God wherever I go.

I receive prophetic revelation and send it forth.

I distribute the love of God to everyone I meet.

No need of mine is too great for my God.

I am gentle, merciful, loving and kind.

I speak peace from my mouth and encourage others.

I Am Not Defeated!

I am not defeated. I am more than a conqueror in Christ Jesus!

I am empowered from on high!

I break agreement with a poverty, victim and defeat mentality, in Jesus' name.

My identity is not in lack, negativity, or as a pauper.

I am a Son of God, and my identity is in Christ.

My mind is renewed, transformed, sound, full of knowledge and empowered!

Jesus defeated it all on the cross; therefore, my defeat went to the grave, so I can rise victorious as Jesus did.

My mentality is not dictated by my circumstances, I live by faith, not by sight or emotion.

I command my ungodly soulish tendencies to leave now, in Jesus' name!

I will walk in the Spirit, not the flesh.

I am changing behavior and thought patterns for the glory of the Kingdom.

I choose to put on joy and walk in love.

My love for God and His people will prevail and not selfish ambition.

I will walk in His plan and destiny and not my own.

I call those things that are held up in the spiritual realm over my life to manifest that are according to God's will, in Jesus' name.

I Have a Sound Mind

I have a sound mind.
    My mind thinks right.
My mind thinks good thoughts.
    My mind is solid.
My mind is steadfast.
    I think on thoughts from above.
I think on positive things.
    I have spiritual thoughts.
I have encouraging thoughts.
    I have a sound mind.
I have prosperous thoughts.
    I take hold of my imagination.
My imagination does not run wild.
    Vain imaginations are not in my mind.
I have a sound mind; my mind belongs to God.
    I hold every thought captive.
I bind my mind to the mind of Christ.
    Peace runs through my mind.
Worry is a thing of the past.
    Fear is nonexistent in my mind.
Concern is canceled in my mind.
    I cancel spirits that would lie to me and tell me anything else.
My mind is right.
    It thinks good thoughts.
I have a sound mind.

I Have the Power

I have the power of:

    Intelligence

    Leadership

    Creativity

    Inventions

    Ideas

    Investments

    Hearing

    Listening

    Healing

    Miracles

    Prophecy

    Concepts

    Understanding

    Knowledge

    Wisdom

    Wealth

    Partnership

I Speak Life

I speak life.

I speak health.

I speak wholeness.

I speak love.

I believe for healing.

I believe I am righteous.

I have hope.

I have faith.

I have a strong belief system in the One who loves us, in the One who created us, and in the One who made us. He created us in His image, in His likeness.

He made us new and to be renewed in Him—just like Him.

Like Him I am, in His image.

I am like Him.

I am in Him, and He in us, together with Him, together in Him, forever.

I Trust

Today I claim, command and decree that I trust.

    I trust God for the unseen.

I choose to walk in faith.

    I choose to believe the best.

God's got my back.

    He isn't going to let me go.

I'm moving forward in the area of trust.

    I'm giving up the past and moving forward.

I'm trusting my Heavenly Father.

    I will live in the truth of His love.

I'm trusting.

    I'm trusting Him for the future.

Leaving the past behind.

    Leaving the hurt behind.

Leaving the distrust behind.

    I am choosing to live in the light of His love.

I'm choosing to move forward for His glory and for my freedom in the light of His love.

Peace

I have peace like a river.
>It flows through my veins.

It permeates to every part of me.
>In my path is peace.

Great peace.
>There is stillness in my path.

I meditate on God's Word.
>It brings me peace.

My mouth speaks peace.
>My mind thinks peace.

My body feels peace.
>I live in the peace of His presence.

I live in the tabernacle of peace.
>This is my confession.

I believe and receive peace.
>This is my prophecy over myself.

I believe in peace.
>I believe I can have what I say I can have, and I say I have peace.

It permeates my soul.
>I live in the peaceful river of God.

Peace is mine.
>I have it. I have it.

THERE ARE THINGS we suffer from such as fear, rejection, anger, depression and other topical issues. As the previous proclamations declared out trust, peace, faith, blessings and other positive things, take a moment and write down what you struggle with and write a declaration against the very thing that has been a stronghold in your life.

My Personal Declaration to Bring Me to a Place of Freedom

_____

_____

_____

_____

_____

_____

_____

_____

_____

_____

_____

Powerful Prophetic Declarations

Powerful Prophetic Declarations

My Proclamation of Joy!

POWERFUL PROPHETIC DECLARATIONS

My Proclamation of Perseverance!

My Proclamation
for Keeping Focused and Balanced

POWERFUL PROPHETIC DECLARATIONS

My Proclamation of Patience and Rest

Anointing and Wisdom
I Claim, Call Forth and Release...

Prophetic insights and revelation...

The Kingdom to be established in me...

Prophetic wisdom...

People and ministries to co-labor with me...

Apostolic instruction to go forth...

Financial partnerships and increase...

Healing to come forth in my body...

Strength to be in abundance—physically, spiritually, emotionally...

Entrepreneurs and business people to share ideas, wisdom and finances for Kingdom co-laboring and advancement...

Ministry doors to open—abundantly...

Creative strategies for business and ministry...

Book publishing contracts...

Focus and clarity in my mind...

Healing in my heart—physical or emotional...

Wisdom in my finances...

Abundant love to flow through me...

Productivity in my day...

Fresh oil and increased anointing...

Rivers of the living waters to flow through me...

Understanding and comprehension of the Scriptures...

I Am Will Accept My Assignment!

I will accept my calling.

I am worthy of the assignment God put on my life.

I am not jealous of another person's gifts because God has also anointed me.

I come against backlash from the enemy for my assignment.

I am going to complete my Godly task with all diligence.

My hope and foundation are in the Lord.

I do not rely on myself but am empowered by the Holy Spirit.

I have more than enough because the Holy Spirit resides in me.

I am life because Jesus is life, and His resurrection power lives in me.

My God is the hope for tomorrow when all hope seems gone because He is the God of hope.

Kingdom Destiny

I'm going to preach to the nations and set their hearts ablaze for God.

I'm going to distribute the fire of God to encourage, inspire and ignite people to prophesy!

I'm going to impact everyone I come in contact with and stir up a hunger and desire in that person's soul that can't be satisfied.

I'm going to use creative ability led by the Holy Spirit's inspiration to lead people to the Lord.

In these last days, I will not be found idle or downtrodden. The joy of the Lord is my strength, and I have more than enough to accomplish my tasks.

His portion is my inheritance, and I'm taking my inheritance and manifesting the Kingdom out of me here on earth.

Nothing and no one is getting in my path and obstructing obstacles to my Kingdom assignment. I bind and restrict enemy assignments and fleshly opposition.

New things are coming my way; His plans and purposes and spiritual positions.

I am more than victorious and a conqueror. I am developed and equipped for my Kingdom task. I do not lack in anything He wants me to accomplish.

Movement—good movement, right movement—in the spiritual realm is happening on my behalf with angels dispatched, awakened, alert and activated on their assignments.

New things, new places and new people I will impact and ignite.

I'm released into my assignment, and I'm taking it by force. I cover it in the blood of Jesus and destroy, abolish and utterly cut off evil forces set against it, in Jesus' name!

I seal it in and prophesy it to come forth!

Spouse's Ministry Assignment

My spouse will be a strong teacher of the Word.

My spouse will walk in, and own with humility, his prophetic destiny.

My spouse will support me in my ministry calling with unity and love.

I proclaim my spouse's anointing is increasing for the glory of God.

I declare my spouse to receive a deeper understanding of the Scriptures.

My spouse will exude love, God's love in each moment, situation and circumstance.

In my life, my spouse and I will glorify the Father and His Kingdom together.

I decree repentance and change for my spouse's passivity and complacency for the Kingdom.

I call forth ministry assignments for my spouse separate from me.

Father God, break down the walls and allow Your love to be received into his heart in Your fullness.

Meetings

I command no weapon formed against these meetings to prosper, in Jesus' name.

I bind any and all demonic influence who have been sent to interrupt this meeting, in Jesus' name.

I say that our prayer time will be protected, guarded and covered with the blood of Christ and angelic servants.

I bind the demonic realm from hearing my prayers and prophecies and activating on them, in Jesus' name.

I call forth the Spirit of the living God to saturate this meeting with His presence and His love, in Jesus' name!

I bless You, Lord, for what You are going to do here today, and I invite You, Holy Spirit, to come in and have Your way. Come in and teach, instruct and discipline today.

Lord, I come here today to worship Your holy and reverential name.

Receive my praises as a sweet offering at Your throne.

I come here today to love on You.

I adore You, Jesus; You are my everything, the love of my life.

Accept my praises today.

I am here to worship You in freedom, spirit and truth, in Jesus' name.

Kingdom Faith

Claim out this declaration of who you are in the Kingdom and for the great faith that is going to manifest out of you!

I declare and decree my faith will be daily exhibited.

I proclaim I am a servant to the King.

I call forth the love and power of God to be released to all I come in contact.

The resurrection power of Jesus lives in me to pray healing and see it manifest!

The love of God permeates me!

I draw from a free, flowing well of the living water in Christ.

I am new in Him!

His Word is my identity!

I am one with the Word, and the Word is one with me!

The Kingdom manifests out of me every moment!

I am overflowing with the joy of the Lord!

I am energized and strengthened to walk in the anointing all the time!

I am about My Father's business, which is Kingdom business.

Life flows from me, abundantly!

I lovingly serve the Lord and people with excess from the throne of God.

W<small>E CAN PROPHESY</small> and speak and decree over our lives. We do not need to wait for a prophet to speak over us when we can hear clearly from the Lord. Every year I encourage the people who receive from my teaching to write a prophetic word over themselves for the year. On these pages, write a prophetic proclamation prophesying over yourself and what you desire to see happen in your life.

Powerful Prophetic Declarations

Powerful Prophetic Declarations

Powerful Prophetic Declarations

Powerful Prophetic Declarations

Health ~ Healing

I decree and declare health and healing to come into my body right now!
I live in divine health!
I am life because Jesus is life, and Jesus lives in me!
Sickness and disease cannot and will not live in my body!
I have been given a blood transfusion, and the blood of Jesus exists in my veins and is running to every tissue and organ producing life and health.
I will live by my heavenly Father's Word and not by a doctor's report.
I come against doctors' reports and in the mighty name of Jesus, I speak against any diagnosis given that does not line up with the Word of God.
I claim the scriptures that Christ heals all and every time, and I call forth that divine healing He purchased on the cross for me.
I rebuke the devourer and call my body into the light of God's love.
I claim I am healed, whole, delivered and set free from any and all physical infirmity.
Cancer cannot exist in my body.
Estrogen levels will be normal, in Jesus' name.
Clarity of mind will exist.
Confusion will not attack my mind or body.
The blood of Jesus runs through my veins.
I am equipped for every good work of the Lord.
I live in victory.
I am happy, joyful, peaceful and expecting good things.
I live healed!

Physical Healing

I speak life into my body.

I command my mind, will and emotions to line up with my spirit-man and be healed.

I command all oppression to leave my body.

Heart beat right, blood pressure be 120 over 80.

Blood purify.

T-cells eat up any cancer attempting to invade my body.

I command gall bladders, pancreata and livers to work properly and all kidneys to produce waste.

I say I have a sound mind; my mind thinks right thoughts.

Negativity must go.

Pain cannot and will not exist in my body.

No demonic invasion in my body, in Jesus' name.

The blood of Jesus runs through my veins.

Healing and prosperity are mine.

I am life because Jesus is life, and He lives in me.

My body is growing stronger every day.

My body loses fat and maintains proper body weight.

Muscle is growing inside my body.

My body releases germs, sickness and disease.

With long life, I will live.

My body will serve the Lord.

Strength, come to me now.

Health, come into my body.

Body, line up to the word of God.

I command healing to go forth to every part of my body.

By His stripes, I am healed, in Jesus' name.

Infertility

I command my body to be fruitful and multiply.

All blockages, I command you to open.

I call forth eggs to release on a timely basis and connect with sperm.

I call forth my uterus to work properly, in Jesus' name.

I say leave infertility, delay and lack of conception, in Jesus' name.

My bloodline and the bloodline of my children are covered in the blood of Jesus.

I command children to be produced from my womb.

I thank You, Lord, that You fearfully and wonderfully made me in my mother's womb, and I command that miracle-working power to go throughout my womb right now.

I command my husband's male parts to be strong and work properly. Sperm get to your destination, in Jesus' name.

I call forth divine intervention in my womb.

I thank You, Father, that You created life and designed life for my womb.

I thank You that my womb is strong and healthy and can carry several children to full term.

God, as You opened Rachel's womb, I speak to my womb, and I say be opened by the power of God.

God's Word says the fruit of my womb will be blessed; womb, produce fruit and life!

I come against the enemy and say you will not destroy the destiny of any future child of mine by not producing life. You will not destroy my marriage by having dissension and irritation through infertility problems.

I will have no miscarriages or premature deaths, in Jesus' name!

No weapon formed against my womb and child bearing will prosper!

I call forth life in abundance and that my children will serve the Lord all the days of their lives, in Jesus' powerful, mighty name.

Jesus healed the sick. Throughout the Gospels, we read stories of how He brought forth the ministry of healing and deliverance. Speaking to our body parts and telling them to come into alignment with the Word of God and to manifest their healing is powerful. Write your own healing declarations based on scriptural fact and telling those organs to work in the perfection God created them. Command your physical ailments to be reversed and for health to manifest in your body.

Powerful Prophetic Declarations

Powerful Prophetic Declarations

Powerful Prophetic Declarations

Finances

Blessing and favor are mine.

Prosperity is coming in abundance.

I speak to lack and poverty, and I say no more.

Revelation and business ideas for financial growth are coming my way.

Entrepreneurship is my destiny.

Hobbies come forth to business ideas.

My faith will grow now in Jesus' name.

Renewed strength come into my body to accomplish all of the plans God has for me.

Partnerships come.

Debt, go! Be paid off! Erased!

Financial lack, be abolished!

Devil, you are cut off from my finances!

Poverty mindset, you are gone.

Victim mentality, be removed.

Sound mind and creative ideas come forth.

There is no lack for people in the Kingdom, and since I am in the Kingdom, I have no lack.

God, help me to be a giver in my lack so I can go forth and give in abundance.

Tithe/Offering
by Pastor Ron DeGraw

I sow my financial seed into the Kingdom.

I declare and decree that I am no longer under the curse.

I sow my seed in faith and in the promises of God.

I declare freedom from the world's economy and lack.

I speak the word of faith over my seed that, as I walk according to the Word and obey God's Word, He will make my way prosperous, and I will have good success.

I say that everything I do will prosper.

I thank You, Lord, that You have blessed me so that I can be a blessing to others.

I claim this seed to be prosperous, and as I sow, I will increase even more.

I speak this all in Jesus' name.

Sale of a Home

I call forth the perfect buyers for my house.

    Lord, have the buyers for my house put their house on the market.

I command the finances to come forth for the buyers of my home.

    I dispatch angels on assignment to sell my home.

Expose and highlight my house on the listings.

    I call forth my realtor to work on my behalf.

I command my house to sell for full market price or above.

    I cover the sale and transaction with the blood of Christ.

The Bible frequently addressed the matter of finances. God desires us to live in prosperity. Write a proclamation claiming and decreeing that your debts are paid in full and that you are debt-free. Command your checking and savings accounts to increase. Speak to your paycheck and tell your salary to increase.

Powerful Prophetic Declarations

My Financial Declaration

Powerful Prophetic Declarations

Powerful Prophetic Declarations

A LACK OF finances and debt hold people in bondage and a poverty and lack mentality. Write a proclamation to change your mind and way of thinking and call forth that you are a giver.

Powerful Prophetic Declarations

Powerful Prophetic Declarations

My Financial Declaration Changing My Way of Thinking When It Comes to Finances

Powerful Prophetic Declarations

My Financial Declaration Calling Forth that I Am a Giver!

Powerful Prophetic Declarations

Powerful Prophetic Saturation

I call forth the love of God to manifest in me.

Overwhelm me, Lord, with Your presence and love. Let me experience You!

I call forth a saturation of His presence to permeate my life, home and workplace.

I proclaim He will use me as a mighty vessel, overflowing with the goodness of His pleasure.

I say everything I do will prosper, and God's Word will be sent forth in my life.

I command the heavens to open and angels to activate and be dispatched on my behalf.

I order and instruct a fresh heavenly rain to fall upon me, drawing me into a place of shalom and tranquility with Him.

I establish God's order in my life and command all chaos to dissipate, in Jesus' name.

I proclaim this will be a day established in the Lord that I will remember where change manifested, freedom occurred, and the opportunities God has written for me will manifest.

I seal this prophetic decree in and call it forth for my life today in the name of Jesus, by the blood of the Lamb, and in the power and love of our Father God!

Releasing the Past

I am moving forward!

    Old habits and behavior patterns, I leave you behind.

I break agreement with offense, anger and rejection in my life!

    All ungodly soul ties and relationships will no longer affect me.

I am no longer a victim, but I am victorious!

    The provision for my destiny will come forth!

Divine connections for ministry appointments manifest!

    My mind is full of truth, and no lies of the enemy will infiltrate it!

Depression is gone; joy every morning will come!

    I speak the word of God, life and health into my body.

I am healed by His stripes.

    I am a giver and will have more than enough to disperse.

I will saturate others in God's love at all times.

    My dreams and desires will come forth!

I will gain much spiritual growth.

    Favor, blessing and abundance are mine, in Jesus' name!

Prophetic Fulfillment Come Forth!

I call forth every vision and prophetic fulfillment according to the Word of God for my life, in Jesus' name.

I command the Word of God to come forth for my life, my family and my finances. My ministry is to be delayed no longer, in Jesus' name.

The word which the Lord has spoken to me shall come to pass, no more postponed, in Jesus' name.

The Lord says the word and performs it over my life, in Jesus' name.

None of God's words, plans, visions and destinies for my life will be postponed any longer, in Jesus' name.

Spirit of God, send forth Your plans and purposes for my life today, in Jesus' name.

I call forth the fulfillment of every Godly vision I've had. My days are here!

The Lord says His word and performs it. The Lord is performing His word on my behalf.

My visions and my prophesies are coming to pass.

Spiritual realm, hear the word of the Lord spoken and activate on my behalf, in Jesus' name.

Victorious!

I shall be victorious!

Every where I step, I shall be prosperous and victorious.

I shall be victorious over my enemies.

I shall be victorious in my business and ministry.

No weapon formed against me shall prosper; I will be victorious.

No curses shall rise against me; I will be victorious.

No emotional bondage shall plague me; I shall be victorious.

No tongue shall speak against me, my family, business or ministry.

I will not be intimidated; I will be victorious.

I declare and decree health and healing to come into my body.

I say declarations and decrees come forth easily and with speed.

I speak to the dry bones and dead areas of my life to come to life and come forth that are according to the will of God.

Areas that are dry and dead and unfruitful and unproductive that will strain and distract me, be removed, according to God's will.

I call forth ministry connections and appointments to come forth speedily and with confirmation, according to God's will.

I declare the mountains and obstacles in my life to crumble, in Jesus' name.

We are conquerors and victorious. We have an inheritance in heaven! Our identity is in Christ. Write a proclamation claiming all that you are and all that you want to be.

Powerful Prophetic Declarations

Powerful Prophetic Declarations

Powerful Prophetic Declarations

Powerful Prophetic Declarations

Worship

I proclaim and announce this will be a day of worship to the King.

I call forth the glory of God to descend while I worship.

I say I will worship in freedom and truth without distractions!

I bind distractions from entering and plaguing my worship time.

My worship time will be holy and pure—not infected with unclean thoughts.

I thank You, Lord, that I can approach Your throne of grace in which to receive mercy in the time of need.

Lord, let my praises be sweet to You.

I will bless the Lord at all times.

I thank You, Lord, that I have energy and strength in my body.

I claim new revelation will come forth while I worship.

I call forth intimacy with the Father, communion with Him while I lift my hands in praise and adoration to the King.

May His name be blessed!

Amen!

Widespread Declaration

I proclaim the devil and his cohorts will be under my feet as it is stated in the Bible it should be.

I say I will rise up and take the authority Jesus gave to me.

No worry, no fear, no doubt and no burden bearing will attack or plague me, in Jesus' name.

My health and the health of my family will be perfect and complete. Our bodies will not malfunction. They will produce abundant life.

I command business ideas, investments and a mind of entrepreneurship to come forth. I thank You, God, for the creative ideas are coming my way.

I plead the blood of Jesus over my family, team, ministries and children.

I call forth my children and spouse to fall more in love with You, Jesus, and to serve the Lord all the days of their life.

I say this year I will eat healthy, and my body will lose fat.

I call forth the glory of the Lord to be established and released in those I love and throughout the earth.

I say and commit to doing my part this year to desecrate racism.

My mind, my thoughts will be complete in Him, lacking nothing. My mind will not wander or stray with vain imaginations but will be continually focused on Him and His goodness.

I claim this will be a year that my storehouses will overflow.

I call forth this year will be a fruitful year for the Kingdom and that my tree will yield much fruit.

I call forth the vault of heaven to open on my behalf. May the vault of revelation be open to me to feast from.

I proclaim this will be a year that the past sins in my mind would truly be erased.

May the abundance of heaven drop on me like dewdrops of rain.

I purpose and plan to study the Word of God daily and to allow it to ignite me.

I originate from God, and since I have His DNA, I will act like Him.

Every dark path in my life will now shine with the light of God.

I pronounce this to be a year of release of good things in my life and ministry in the name of Jesus.

Powerful Prophetic Declarations

Powerful Prophetic Declarations

Powerful Prophetic Declarations

Powerful Prophetic Declarations

Powerful Prophetic Declarations

About the Author

Kathy DeGraw is the founder and president of DeGraw Ministries, a prophetic healing and deliverance ministry releasing the love and power of God. She travels internationally, imparting into believers and igniting them to release their full potential.

She is passionate about serving and loving God and people in every action. She brings her Be Love Prophetic Tours around the U.S., ministering through street evangelism and empowering believers at the Holy Spirit's leading.

Kathy is the author of Speak Out, Flesh, Satan or God, Time to Set the Captives Free, Warfare Declarations, A Worship-Woven Life, and The Sky's the Limit. She has been a regular contributor to Charisma Magazine and was a featured author in Charisma Media's "Life in the Spirit" series.

Kathy is passionate about bridging the divide of racism through her corporation Change Into Colorless. Her desire is to bring forth healing, unity and love.

Kathy is married to her best friend, Pastor Ron DeGraw. They co-pastor Ruach Ha'Kodesh Apostolic Empowerment Center. She is mom to three adult children, Dillon, Amber, and Lauren. They reside in Grandville, Michigan.

To inquire about booking Kathy
for a speaking engagement contact:

DeGraw Ministries
P.O. Box 65 • Grandville, Michigan 49468
Phone: 616-249-8071
Website: www.degrawministries.org
Email: admin@degrawministries.org

Additional Books by Kathy DeGraw

A Worship-Woven Life
(Tate Publishing)

Time to Set the Captives Free
(Westbow Press)

Flesh, Satan or God?
(Westbow Press)

The Sky's the Limit: Creating an Amazing Kids' Club
(CSS Publishing)

Warfare Declarations
(K Publishing)

Baptism of Fire and Power
(K Publishing)

Speak Out
(Creation House)

Made in the USA
Middletown, DE
14 April 2019